alphabet cooking

quadrille

S

is for sri lankan

recipes by rukmini iyer
photography by kim lightbody

S is for Sri Lankan contains 50 of the most definitive

and delicious recipes in modern Sri Lankan cooking.

S is for Sri Lankan ingredients

banana leaves are used as plates in parts of Sri Lanka as the leaves are large, waterproof and flexible. You can buy these from specialist shops

brown mustard seeds are widely used in Asian cooking, and when fried, impart a nutty flavour

curry leaves are dark green, shiny, fragrant leaves from a tree belonging to the citrus family. They have a nutty flavour when fried in oil. Try to use fresh leaves if you can find them

fenugreek seeds are used as a spice and have a sharp pungent taste

ghee is clarified butter and has a high smoke point with a nutty flavour

gram flour is also called chickpea flour and is made from ground chickpeas. It is good for making flatbreads and coating foods, such as pakoras

jackfruit is grown all over South and Southeast Asia. It has a distinctive sweet, fruity smell. In Sri Lanka it is used in curries as it has a meat-like texture when it is young and unripe

jaggery is an unrefined sugar made from cane sugar that has been reduced down and set into blocks. It imparts a rich flavour to dishes

Maldive fish is boiled, smoked and dried tuna produced in the Maldives and is used in cooking for its distinctive flavour. If you can't find it use shrimp paste or fish sauce instead

palm sugar is made from the sap of the sugar palm and adds a rich and creamy sweetness to curries and desserts

rice flour is made from ground raw rice and is used to make appams

string hopper press is used to make string hoppers, a traditional breakfast dish in Sri Lanka. The string hoppers are usually served with a coconut broth

tamarind is a fruit shaped like a long bean. It has a tart, sour, sweet flavour and is used as a key ingredient in curries

turmeric is a bright yellow spice with lots of health benefits and is a major ingredient in curries. Use carefully as it stains

urad dhal is made from black lentils. When the lentils are skinned and split they are creamy white. They are high in fibre and are used in lentil fritters

(Some Sri Lankan ingredients are available from large supermarkets or specialist Asian grocery shops. However, it is also worth checking online through suppliers such as spicesofindia.co.uk or theasiancookshop.co.uk)

(snacks and spices)

dhal
fritters
(ulundhu vadai)

makes **10**

prep

soak **x4**

cook

ingredients
220g (7¾oz/generous 1 cup)
   white urad dhal lentils, washed
5cm (2in) ginger, peeled
   and minced
2 green chillies, deseeded
   and minced
5 curry leaves
1 tsp salt

1 litre (32fl oz/4½ cups)
   vegetable oil, for frying

soak
Cover the lentils with twice their volume in warm water and leave to soak for 4 hours.

blitz
Rinse the lentils and drain, then blitz in a food processor to a thick, dough-like paste. Add the ginger, chillies, curry leaves and salt and mix.

roll
Line a tray with clingfilm (plastic wrap). Using wet hands, break off large walnut-sized portions of the dough and roll into 10 balls. Make a hole in the middle of each one and place on the prepared tray.

deep-fry
Heat the oil in a large wok to 160°C (320°F), then reduce the heat to medium. Fry the fritters in batches of 2 for 5 minutes on each side until golden brown and crisp. Drain on a plate lined with kitchen paper (paper towel). Serve hot.

tamil street food snack

(murukku)

serves

prep

cook

ingredients

160g (5¾oz/1¼ cups) rice flour
140g (5oz/generous 1 cup)
   gram flour
½ tsp salt
¼ tsp chilli powder
¼ tsp bicarbonate of soda
   (baking soda)

1 litre (32fl oz/4½ cups)
   vegetable oil, for frying

mix
Mix the flours, salt, chilli powder and bicarbonate of soda in a bowl. Gradually add 150ml (5fl oz/⅔ cup) water and bring together to form a dough.

heat
Heat the oil in a large wok to 180°C (355°F), making sure to fill it no more than half full.

press
Transfer small sections of the dough to a murukku/ string hopper press using a star-shaped plate attachment, and carefully press out 2–3 circles of dough directly into the hot oil. Do not overfill the pan.

fry
Fry for 2–3 minutes until golden brown and crisp, then drain on a plate lined with kitchen paper (paper towel). Repeat. Store in an airtight container for 3–4 days.

samosas

ingredients

300g (10½oz/2¼ cups)
  plain (all-purpose) flour
1 tsp salt
45ml (1½fl oz/3 Tbsp)
  vegetable oil
300g (10½oz) potatoes,
  peeled and cut into 1-cm
  (½-in) chunks
2 Tbsp vegetable oil
5 curry leaves
2 cloves garlic, peeled
  and minced
2.5cm (1in) ginger, minced
1 leek, thinly sliced
1½ Tbsp Sri Lankan curry
  powder (see page 35)
½ tsp chilli powder
1 tsp salt

mix

Mix the flour and salt together in a large bowl,
then add the oil and 125ml (4fl oz/½ cup) water
and bring together into a stiff dough. Knead briefly
for a few minutes on a work surface. Return to
the bowl, cover with clingfilm (plastic wrap) and
leave to rest at room temperature for 30 minutes.

simmer

Bring a pan of salted water to the boil. Add
the potatoes and simmer for 12 minutes, or
until just cooked. Drain and allow the potatoes
to steam-dry for 5 minutes.

cook

Meanwhile, heat the oil in a large frying pan,
add the curry leaves, garlic and ginger and stir-fry
for 30 seconds. Add the leek and stir-fry for 5–6
minutes until it has softened. Add the curry powder,
chilli powder, salt and peas and stir-fry for 1 minute.

makes

prep

cook

100g (3½oz/scant 1 cup)
   frozen peas, defrosted
juice of ½ lime

1 litre (32fl oz/4½ cups)
   vegetable oil, for frying

stir

Gently stir the leek mixture through the potatoes.
Season as needed with a little more salt and the
lime juice.

roll

Divide the dough into 8 equal portions and roll
each into a circle no thicker than 2mm (¹⁄₁₆in). Place
a heaped tablespoon of the filling inside each
circle of dough, dampen the edges of the pastry
with water, then fold one edge over the filling, then
two more to form a triangle. Repeat until all the
samosas are made.

deep-fry

Heat the oil in a deep saucepan to 180°C (355°F).
Carefully add 2–3 samosas at a time into the hot
oil and deep-fry for 5 minutes, turning frequently,
until golden brown and crisp. Drain on a plate lined
with kitchen paper (paper towel) and repeat until
all the samosas are fried. Serve hot.

vegetable
roti

serves

prep

rest **x2**

cook

ingredients

275g (9¾oz/2 cups) plain
 (all-purpose) flour
2 tsp salt
40ml (3 Tbsp) vegetable oil
400g (14oz) small potatoes,
 unpeeled and halved
2 Tbsp vegetable oil
1 Tbsp mustard seeds
10 curry leaves
2 cloves garlic, minced
2.5cm (1in) ginger, peeled
 and minced
1 green chilli, deseeded
 and finely sliced
1 leek, thinly sliced

mix

Mix the flour and 1 teaspoon salt together, then
add 150ml (5fl oz/⅔ cup) water and bring together
into a stiff pliable dough. Divide the dough into 8
equal balls, dip each into the oil, then cover and
set aside at room temperature for 2 hours.

mash

Meanwhile, bring a pan of salted water to the boil,
add the potatoes and cook for 15 minutes, or until
tender. Drain, allow to cool, then peel and mash.

stir-fry

Heat the oil in a frying pan on a medium heat, add
the mustard seeds, curry leaves, garlic, ginger and
chilli and stir-fry for a few seconds until the mustard
seeds pop. Add the leek and 1 teaspoon salt and
stir-fry for 5–6 minutes until the leek has softened.
Mix with the potatoes.

roll

Roll the dough balls out to no more than 1mm
(1⁄32in) thick, then place 2 heaped tablespoons
of filling inside each. Wrap the dough around
the filling in a square parcel. Repeat with the
rest of the filling and dough.

fry

Heat a large dry frying pan over a medium
heat, add 2–3 parcels at a time and dry-fry
for 4 minutes on each side until golden brown
and crisp. Remove and repeat until all the parcels
are cooked. Serve hot.

fish
cutlets

ingredients

350g (12¼oz) small
　potatoes, unpeeled
1 Tbsp vegetable oil
1 small onion, minced
1 green chilli, deseeded
　and minced
2 cloves garlic, minced
2.5cm (1in) ginger, peeled
　and minced
1 tsp salt
1 Tbsp Sri Lankan curry
　powder (see page 35)
100g (3½oz) smoked
　mackerel, flaked

simmer

Bring a large pan of water to the boil. Add the
potatoes and simmer for 15–20 minutes until just
cooked through. Drain, peel while warm, then
return to the pan, mash roughly and set aside.

fry

Meanwhile, heat the oil in a frying pan on a medium
heat. Add the onion, chilli, garlic, ginger and salt
and fry for 10 minutes, stirring occasionally until
evenly golden brown. Add the curry powder and
stir-fry for a further 2 minutes.

roll

Stir the spiced onion through the potatoes, then
stir through the mackerel. Taste and season the
mixture as needed with more salt. Allow the mixture
to cool, then break off walnut-sized portions of the
mixture and roll into cutlets (balls).

1 litre (32fl oz/4½ cups)
vegetable oil, for frying
1 egg, beaten
50g (1¾oz/scant ⅔ cup)
dried breadcrumbs

chilli sauce or ketchup,
to serve

heat
Heat the oil in a deep saucepan for frying to 180°C
(355°F), or until a cube of bread dropped in fizzes
and turns golden brown within 30 seconds.

coat
Put the beaten egg in a bowl and spread the
breadcrumbs out on a plate. Dip each fish cutlet
into the beaten egg, then into the breadcrumbs
until they are coated all over.

deep-fry
Working in small batches and being careful not
to overfill the pan, carefully drop the cutlets into
the hot oil and deep-fry for 2–3 minutes until
golden brown. Remove them with a slotted spoon
and drain on a plate lined with kitchen paper
(paper towel). Repeat until all the cutlets are fried.
Serve immediately with chilli sauce or ketchup.

fish cutlets

kottu roti

06

kottu roti

ingredients

4 parathas (see page 122
 or frozen bought parathas)
2 Tbsp vegetable oil
10 curry leaves
2 cloves garlic, minced
5cm (2in) ginger, peeled
 and minced
1 green chilli, deseeded
 and finely sliced
1 leek, finely chopped
1 carrot, finely julienned
200g (7oz/3 cups) chestnut
 (cremini) mushrooms,
 finely chopped
2 eggs
1 Tbsp Sri Lankan curry
 powder (see page 35)
4–5 Tbsp leftover chicken
 or beef curry (see pages
 74 and 82), optional

salt or soy sauce, to taste

slice

Roll the parathas up and finely slice them into
strips. Turn the strips around, then chop into
evenly tiny pieces. Set aside.

stir-fry

Heat the oil in a large wok on a medium heat.
Add the curry leaves, garlic, ginger and chilli
and stir-fry for a few seconds. Add the leek,
carrot and mushrooms and stir-fry for a further
2–3 minutes until just wilted.

scramble

Add the eggs and mix briefly to scramble. Add
the curry powder and stir-fry for a further 30
seconds, before adding the chopped parathas
and leftover chicken or beef curry, if using.

mix

Stir-fry for a further 4–5 minutes until everything
is hot all the way through and well mixed. Add
salt or soy sauce to taste. Serve immediately.

egg hoppers
(appam)

serves

prep

ferment **over-night**

cook each

ingredients

400ml (13½fl oz/1⅔ cups)
  coconut water at room
  temperature
1½ tsp fast-action dried
  (active dry) yeast
½ tsp sugar
300g (10½oz/2⅓ cups) rice flour
60ml (2fl oz/¼ cup) coconut milk
½ tsp salt

6 tsp vegetable oil
6 eggs

rise

Mix the coconut water, yeast and sugar, then
pour into the flour. Mix well, cover and leave to
rise for 8 hours, or overnight at room temperature.

stir

Just before you are ready to make the hoppers,
stir through the coconut milk, salt and enough
water to make a thin pancake batter, about the
consistency of double (heavy) cream.

heat

Pour 1 teaspoon of oil into a small, non-stick frying
pan (or hopper pan) and heat on a medium heat.

cook

Pour in enough batter to just cover the base. Swirl
the pan quickly to bring the batter up over the sides.
Crack in an egg, and cook for 5 minutes on a
medium heat until the base is golden and crispy.
Repeat with the remaining batter and eggs. Serve
immediately with the coconut sambol (see page 46).

note

If you don't have a hopper pan you will need
a very good non-stick pan or small wok.

string hoppers

string hoppers

(idiyappam)

serves ● ● ● ●

prep ◕

cook ◑

ingredients

1 tsp salt
1 tsp coconut milk
320g (11¼oz/2½ cups) rice flour
5–6 Tbsp grated fresh coconut

boil

Bring 550ml (19⅓fl oz/2¼ cups) water, the salt and coconut milk to the boil in a large saucepan. Add the rice flour and leave without stirring for 1 minute.

stir

Stir the flour and water together on a medium heat until the water is absorbed into the flour, then cover and leave to steam for 5 minutes.

knead

Transfer the piece of rice dough into a sturdy plastic bag, wrap the bag in a tea towel and while still hot, knead for 5 minutes through the bag until you have a soft, smooth dough.

press

Lay out a steamer basket, then place balls of dough into a string hopper press. Press out the noodles in a circular shape over the steamer basket in a single layer.

steam

Sprinkle with grated coconut, then transfer to a steamer pan. Bring 5cm (2in) water to the boil in the pan, then place the steamer basket over the top, cover and steam for 5 minutes. Repeat until all the string hoppers are cooked. Serve with the kiri hodi (see page 99).

note
You may wish to line the steamer basket with oiled baking parchment.

sri lankan omelette

serves

prep

cook

ingredients
25g (1oz/2 Tbsp) butter or ghee
4 curry leaves
1 green chilli, deseeded
    and finely chopped
½ red onion, finely chopped
4 eggs
1 tsp salt
freshly ground black pepper
100g (3½oz/½ cup) tomatoes,
    finely chopped

stir-fry
Heat the butter in a large frying pan on a medium
heat until foaming, then add the curry leaves,
chilli and onion and stir-fry for 6–7 minutes
until softened.

whisk
Meanwhile, whisk the eggs with the salt and black
pepper to taste. Add the tomatoes to the chilli and
onion mixture and stir-fry for a further minute before
adding the eggs. Stir gently, then cook on a low
heat for 5–6 minutes until the top is just set.

fold
Fold the omelette in half and cook for a further
minute. Slide onto a plate and serve hot.

sri lankan curry powder

prep

cook

ingredients

1 Tbsp basmati rice
1 Tbsp cloves
1 Tbsp fennel seeds
1 Tbsp cumin seeds
8 cardamom pods,
  seeds only
1 tsp fenugreek seeds
1 tsp black peppercorns
1 tsp mustard seeds
15 curry leaves
1 cinnamon stick, broken
3 dried red chillies

heat

Place all the ingredients into a large heavy-based saucepan – they should fit in a single layer. Heat on a low heat, stirring frequently, for 10 minutes, or until aromatic.

grind

Tip the mixture onto a plate to cool, then place in a coffee grinder or pestle and mortar in batches and grind to a fine powder.

store

Store in an airtight container for 2–3 months.

sri lankan curry powder

(dhals, sambols and sides)

dhal curry

(parippu)

serves

prep

cook

ingredients

175g (6¼oz/scant 1 cup)
   red split lentils, well rinsed
1 onion, finely sliced
5cm (2in) ginger, peeled
   and minced
3 cloves garlic, minced
1 green chilli, deseeded
   and finely sliced
1 Tbsp Sri Lankan curry
   powder (see page 35)
1 tsp salt
200ml coconut milk (7fl oz/
   scant 1 cup)

2 Tbsp vegetable oil
2 tsp mustard seeds
2–3 dried red chillies
8 curry leaves
juice of ½ lime
salt

cook

Place the lentils, onion, ginger, garlic, green chilli, curry powder and salt in a saucepan and cover with 800ml (28fl oz/3⅓ cups) boiling water. Bring to the boil, then cover and simmer for 30 minutes until the lentils are soft. Stir in the coconut milk, return to the boil, then turn off the heat.

fry

Heat the oil in a small frying pan until very hot. Add the mustard seeds, red chillies and curry leaves and fry until the mustard seeds pop. Pour into the dhal immediately.

taste

Taste the dhal and season as needed with the lime juice and salt. Serve hot.

lentil and tamarind stew

(sambhar)

serves

prep

cook

ingredients

130g (4½oz/1½ cups) tuvar
   dhal lentils (available in Indian
   shops), well rinsed
80g (3oz/½ cup) red split lentils,
   well rinsed
½ tsp fine salt
½ tsp ground turmeric
30g (1oz/2 Tbsp) tamarind
   extract
10 shallots, halved
1 carrot, peeled and finely sliced
2 tsp ground coriander
¼ tsp chilli powder
10–12 curry leaves, torn
1 tsp salt
¼ tsp asafoetida (optional)
1 Tbsp vegetable oil
½ tsp mustard seeds

cook

Place the lentils in a saucepan with 1½ litres
(51fl oz/6½ cups) boiling water, the salt and
turmeric. Bring to the boil, stir, then cover and
simmer for 30 minutes, stirring halfway through
the cooking time.

simmer

Meanwhile, place the tamarind extract, 400ml
(13½fl oz/1⅔ cups) boiling water, shallots and
carrot in a separate saucepan with the spices,
curry leaves, salt and asafoetida. Bring to the
boil, then cover and simmer for 15 minutes.

whisk

After 30 minutes, whisk the cooked lentils, then
tip them into the pan with the vegetables and
tamarind water. Bring to the boil, then turn off
the heat immediately.

fry

Heat the oil in a small frying pan on a medium heat
until very hot. Add the mustard seeds – they should
splutter and pop immediately. Tip into the cooked
stew, then season to taste with salt as needed.

note
Use a pan lid to protect yourself from the hot popping
mustard seeds.

43

lentil and tamarind stew

coconut
sambol

(pol sambol)

serves ●●●●●●●

prep

ingredients

½ onion, roughly chopped
1 tsp crushed dried red chilli
1 tsp Maldive fish or fish sauce
1 tsp salt
juice of ½ lime
100g (3½oz/scant 1½ cups)
   grated fresh coconut

blitz

Place the onion, chilli, Maldive fish or fish sauce, salt and lime juice in a blender, and blitz until you have a smooth paste.

mix

Mix the paste with the grated coconut until it is completely incorporated, then taste and season with more lime juice or salt as needed.

radish sambol

serves

prep ▶ + ◗

ingredients
200g (7oz) radishes, finely sliced
1 tsp salt
½ red onion, very finely sliced
1 green chilli, deseeded and
  finely sliced
3 heaped Tbsp grated fresh
  coconut
juice of 1 lime

soak
Fill a bowl with enough cold water to cover
the radish slices, add the salt and stir to dissolve.
Leave to soak for 15 minutes.

mix
Drain the radish slices well, then mix with the
chilli, grated coconut and lime juice. Season
to taste with more salt and serve immediately.

onion
sambol

(lunu miris)

serves

prep

ingredients
1 Tbsp dried red chillies
2 red onions, roughly chopped
2 tsp lime juice
1 tsp salt

crush
In a pestle and mortar or spice grinder, crush the chillies into a rough powder.

blitz
Place the chilli powder into a food processor along with the onions, lime juice and salt and blitz to a paste. Taste and adjust the salt and lime juice as needed, and serve alongside string hoppers (see page 33) or kiribath (see page 117).

note
Be very careful handling and grinding the chillies, wear gloves if you can.

kale curry

(kale mallung)

serves

prep

cook

ingredients

2 Tbsp vegetable oil
1 Tbsp mustard seeds
½ tsp ground turmeric
5–6 curry leaves
1 red onion, finely sliced
1 red chilli, deseeded and
    finely sliced
200g (7oz) kale leaves, sliced
½ tsp salt
2 Tbsp grated fresh coconut

fry

Heat the oil in a wok on a high heat until very hot, then add the mustard seeds and turmeric. As soon as the mustard seeds start to pop and splutter, add the curry leaves, onion and chilli. Reduce the heat slightly and stir-fry for 5 minutes before adding the kale.

season

Add 2 tablespoons water, then stir-fry for 2–3 minutes until the kale has just wilted and the water has evaporated. Taste and season well with the salt, and stir through the grated coconut just before serving.

kale curry

aubergine pickle

(wambatu moju)

serves

prep

cook

ingredients

300g (10½oz) small aubergine
  (eggplant), cut into rounds
1 tsp salt
½ tsp ground turmeric
250ml (8½fl oz/1 cup)
  vegetable oil, for frying
1 red onion, finely sliced
2 green chillies, deseeded
  and finely sliced
1 Tbsp mustard seeds
2 cloves garlic, finely chopped
1 tsp caster (superfine) sugar
100ml (3½fl oz/7 Tbsp) white
  malt vinegar

rub

Rub the aubergine slices with the salt and turmeric.

deep-fry

Heat the oil in a large wok until very hot. Deep-fry
the aubergine slices in batches for 4–5 minutes
each batch, until golden brown, turning the slices
over once. Drain on a plate lined with kitchen paper
(paper towel) until all the aubergine is cooked.
Deep-fry the red onion in the same oil for 2–3
minutes until crisp, then transfer to separate plate
lined with kitchen paper. Repeat with the green
chillies for 30 seconds until just crisp.

mix

Place the mustard seeds, garlic, sugar and vinegar
in a small saucepan and bring to the boil. Turn
off the heat, then mix with the aubergine, onion and
chillies. Season with salt, cool and serve with rice.

(fish and   seafood curry)

tamarind fish curry

(ambul thiyal)

serves

prep

cook

ingredients

2 Tbsp vegetable oil
1 onion, finely chopped
10 curry leaves
4 cloves
½ tsp fenugreek seeds
1 tsp black peppercorns
1 green chilli, deseeded
  and finely chopped
2 cloves garlic, finely chopped
1 Tbsp Sri Lankan curry
  powder (see page 35)
2 Tbsp tamarind paste
1 tsp salt
2 tuna steaks (approx. 30g/
  1oz each)

stir-fry

Heat the oil in a frying pan on a medium heat and stir-fry the onion and curry leaves for 10 minutes until evenly golden brown.

crush

Meanwhile, crush the cloves, fenugreek seeds and black peppercorns in a pestle and mortar, then pound in the chilli and garlic until it is a smooth paste. Stir in the curry powder, tamarind paste and salt to form a curry paste.

rub

Rub the tuna steaks all over with the curry paste, then add to the onion in the pan. Pour in 30ml (1fl oz/2 tablespoons) water and cook the steaks for 4–5 minutes on each side on a medium–low heat. Serve hot with rice.

chilli fish curry

serves ●●

prep ◕

cook ◑

ingredients

2 Tbsp vegetable oil
1 tsp mustard seeds
10 curry leaves
2 cloves garlic, minced
5cm (2in) ginger, peeled
  and minced
2 green chillies, deseeded
  and finely sliced
1 onion, finely sliced
100g (3½oz/½ cup) tomatoes,
  roughly chopped
200ml (7fl oz/scant 1 cup)
  coconut milk
300g (10½oz) cod or pollock
  fillets, skin removed
1 tsp salt
juice of 1 lime

stir-fry

Heat the oil in a large frying pan on a medium heat, add the mustard seeds, curry leaves, garlic, ginger and chillies and stir-fry for a few seconds until the mustard seeds pop.

cook

Add the onion to the pan and stir-fry on a medium heat for 10 minutes until the onion is softened and golden brown. Add the tomatoes and cook for a further 5 minutes before adding the coconut milk.

simmer

Simmer for 2–3 minutes, then add the fish, scatter with the salt. Spoon the sauce over the fish, cover the pan and cook for 5–6 minutes until the fish is cooked through.

taste

Taste the sauce and season with more salt if needed and the lime juice. Serve with rice.

sweet and sour fish curry

serves

prep

cook

ingredients

300g (10½oz) white fish
  (sea bass or cod), cut into
  5-cm (2-in) pieces
1 tsp salt
½ tsp ground turmeric
1 tsp chilli flakes
3 Tbsp vegetable oil
1 onion, finely sliced
1 clove garlic, minced
2.5cm (1in) ginger, peeled
  and minced
5–6 curry leaves
2 red (bell) peppers,
  roughly chopped
100g (3½oz/½ cup) tomatoes,
  roughly chopped
1 Tbsp soy sauce
1 Tbsp white wine vinegar

mix

Gently mix the fish with the salt, turmeric and
chilli flakes.

fry

Heat the oil in a frying pan on a medium heat and
carefully fry the fish pieces for 2 minutes on each
side until golden brown. Drain on a plate lined with
kitchen paper (paper towel).

stir-fry

Add the onion to the hot oil along with the garlic,
ginger and curry leaves and stir-fry on a medium
heat for 7–8 minutes until golden brown.

mix

Add the red peppers and tomatoes and stir-fry
for a further 5–6 minutes until the peppers are soft.
Add the soy sauce and vinegar, then add the fish
and very gently mix together. Serve hot with rice.

squid curry

serves

prep

cook

ingredients

200g (7oz) squid, cut into rings
½ tsp ground turmeric
1 Tbsp Sri Lankan curry powder
  (see page 35)
2 Tbsp vegetable oil
5–6 curry leaves
1 green chilli, deseeded and
  finely chopped
2 cloves garlic, finely sliced
½ tsp fenugreek seeds
1 onion, finely sliced
200ml (7fl oz/scant 1 cup)
  coconut milk
juice of 1 lime
1 tsp salt

mix

Mix the squid rings with the turmeric and curry powder and set aside.

stir-fry

Heat the oil in a large saucepan on a medium heat, then add the curry leaves, chilli, garlic and fenugreek seeds and stir-fry for a few seconds. Add the onion and stir-fry for 10 minutes until golden brown.

simmer

Add the marinated squid and stir-fry for a further minute before adding the coconut milk. Simmer for 3–4 minutes until the squid is cooked through, then season to taste with the lime juice and salt before serving.

sri lankan prawn curry

serves

prep

cook

ingredients

2 Tbsp vegetable oil
1 onion, finely sliced
2 cloves garlic, minced
1 green chilli, deseeded
  and finely chopped
5–6 curry leaves
½ stick lemongrass, bashed
½ tsp ground turmeric
½ Tbsp Sri Lankan curry
  powder (see page 35)
1 tsp salt
200ml (7fl oz/scant 1 cup)
  coconut milk
225g (8oz) raw tiger prawns
  (shrimp), peeled
juice of 1 lime

stir-fry

Heat the oil in a frying pan on a medium heat,
then add the onion, garlic, chilli, curry leaves
and lemongrass and stir-fry for 10 minutes until
the onion is golden brown.

simmer

Add the turmeric, curry powder and salt, and stir-
fry for a further minute before adding the coconut
milk. Stir well, then add the prawns. Bring to the
boil and simmer for 3–4 minutes until the prawns
are just cooked through.

taste

Taste and season as needed with the lime juice
and more salt. Serve with rice.

devilled prawn curry

serves

prep

cook

ingredients

2 Tbsp vegetable oil

2 cloves garlic, minced

2.5cm (1in) ginger, peeled and minced

1 onion, finely sliced

1 red (bell) pepper, finely sliced

1 yellow (bell) pepper, finely sliced

2 tomatoes, halved and sliced

1 tsp chilli powder (less or more, depending on strength)

1 Tbsp tomato ketchup

360g (12¾oz) raw prawns (shrimp)

1 tsp salt

juice of ½ lime

fry

Heat the oil in a wok, then add the garlic, ginger and onion and stir-fry for 3–4 minutes. Add the red and yellow peppers and tomatoes and fry for a further 5 minutes until the peppers are softened.

stir-fry

Add the chilli powder and ketchup and stir-fry for 30 seconds before adding the prawns. Stir-fry for 2–3 minutes until the prawns are completely pink and cooked through.

season

Season to taste with the salt and lime juice and serve immediately.

(meat curry)

sri lankan burger

sri lankan
burger

(lamprais)

serves

prep

cook

ingredients

200g (7oz/generous 1 cup) long-grain rice, rinsed

360ml (12fl oz/1½ cups) vegetable/chicken stock

2 banana leaves

4 Tbsp coconut milk

6 Tbsp chicken/beef/jackfruit curry (see pages 74, 82 or 88)

4 Tbsp aubergine pickle (see page 54)

4 fish cutlets (see page 20)

2 Tbsp onion sambol (see page 50)

simmer

Place the rice and stock in a saucepan and bring to the boil. Stir, reduce the heat to a low simmer, then cover and cook for 15 minutes. Fluff the rice through and leave, uncovered, to steam-dry for 5 minutes.

heat

Preheat the oven to 200°C/400°F/gas mark 6.

toast

Toast both banana leaves all over on a gas flame for a few seconds to make them more pliable. Place the rice in the centre of each leaf and pour 2 Tbsp coconut milk over each mound of rice.

wrap

Arrange the curry, aubergine pickle, fish cutlets and onion sambol equally around each portion of rice, then package everything up tightly in the banana leaf, tying it up with string or a long strip of banana leaf.

bake

Pop the parcels onto a baking tray and bake for 30 minutes. Carefully unwrap the packages at the table and serve hot.

chicken curry

(kukul mas)

serves ●●●●

prep ●

marinate **x3** or **over-night**

cook **x1**

ingredients

700g (1lb 9oz) skinless chicken
   thighs, halved
2 Tbsp Sri Lankan curry powder
   (see page 35)
2 tsp salt
25g (1oz/2 Tbsp) ghee or butter
1 onion, finely chopped
1 green chilli, deseeded
   and finely chopped
2 cloves garlic, peeled and
   finely chopped
5cm (2in) ginger, finely chopped
½ stick lemongrass, finely
   chopped
1 Tbsp white malt vinegar
200ml (7fl oz/scant 1 cup)
   coconut milk
1 Tbsp tomato purée (paste)
juice of ½ lime
1 bunch coriander (cilantro),
   roughly chopped

marinate

Mix the chicken thighs with the curry powder
and 1 tsp of the salt. Cover and leave to marinate
in the fridge for 3 hours or overnight.

stir-fry

Heat the ghee in a large saucepan on a medium
heat, then add the onion, chilli, garlic, ginger
and lemongrass and stir-fry for 10–12 minutes
until evenly golden brown and soft.

cook

Add the marinated chicken and stir-fry for 2–3
minutes, then add 200ml (7fl oz/scant 1 cup)
water, the remaining salt and the vinegar. Bring
to a very low simmer, then cover and cook
for a further 30 minutes.

stir

Stir through the coconut milk and tomato purée
and simmer, uncovered, for a further 10 minutes.
Taste and season with more salt and the lime
juice as needed. Sprinkle with the coriander
before serving.

chicken curry

sri lankan
goat curry

serves

prep

cook **x2**

ingredients

600g (1lb 5oz) goat or mutton, diced

5cm (2in) ginger, minced

2 cloves garlic, peeled and minced

2 Tbsp Sri Lankan curry powder (see page 35)

1 tsp salt

2 Tbsp vegetable oil

10 curry leaves

1 green chilli, deseeded and finely sliced

½ Tbsp fenugreek seeds

½ stick lemongrass, bashed

1 onion, finely sliced

100g (3½oz/½ cup) canned chopped tomatoes

400ml (13½fl oz/1⅔ cups) coconut milk

mix

Mix the goat with the ginger, garlic, curry powder and salt, and set aside.

stir-fry

Heat the oil in a large ovenproof saucepan on a medium heat, then add the curry leaves, chilli, fenugreek seeds and lemongrass and stir-fry for 30 seconds. Add the onion and cook for 10 minutes, stirring occasionally, until golden brown.

cook

Add the seasoned goat and stir-fry for a further 3–4 minutes before adding the tomatoes. Stir-fry for a further 2–3 minutes, then add the coconut milk. Bring to the boil, reduce the heat to a very low simmer and cook for 2 hours until the meat is falling apart. Alternatively, transfer to an oven preheated to 150°C/300°F/gas mark 2 for 2 hours. Serve hot.

devilled pork

serves

prep

cook

ingredients

600g (1lb 5oz) pork shoulder,
  cut into cubes
25ml (1fl oz/2 Tbsp) white vinegar
1 tsp salt
3 Tbsp vegetable oil
2 large onions, finely chopped
2 green chillies, deseeded
  and finely chopped
5 cloves garlic, finely minced
5cm (2in) ginger, peeled and
  finely minced
10 curry leaves
4 cardamom pods, seeds only
½ tsp fenugreek seeds
1 tsp chilli flakes
1 Tbsp Sri Lankan curry
  powder (see page 35)
4 tomatoes, finely chopped
1 Tbsp soy sauce

mix

Mix the pork with the vinegar and salt. Set aside.

stir-fry

Heat the oil in a saucepan on a medium heat, then add the onions, chillies, garlic, ginger and curry leaves and stir-fry for 10 minutes until golden brown. Add the pork and stir-fry for 5 minutes.

cook

Add the cardamom pods, fenugreek seeds, chilli flakes and curry powder and fry for a further minute before adding the tomatoes. Stir for a further minute, then cover and cook on a very low heat for 30 minutes, stirring occasionally, adding a few tablespoons water if the mixture looks too dry.

season

Stir in the soy sauce and season to taste.

28

beef curry
(kuruma iraichchi)

ingredients

600g (1lb 5oz) stewing
  beef, diced
1 Tbsp freshly ground
  black pepper
1 Tbsp Sri Lankan curry
  powder (see page 35)
1 tsp salt
2 Tbsp vegetable oil
10 curry leaves
5cm (2in) ginger,
  peeled and minced
3 cloves garlic, minced
1 green chilli, deseeded
  and finely chopped
1 onion, finely sliced
½ tsp ground turmeric
300ml (10fl oz/1¼ cups)
  coconut milk

mix

Mix the beef with the black pepper, curry powder
and salt. Set aside.

cook

Heat the oil in an ovenproof saucepan or casserole
dish on a medium heat, then add the curry leaves,
ginger, garlic and chilli and stir-fry for a few seconds.
Add the onion and cook, stirring occasionally, for
10 minutes, or until golden brown.

stir-fry

Add the turmeric and stir-fry for a further 30
seconds. Add the beef and stir-fry for 2–3 minutes.

boil

Pour in the coconut milk and bring to the boil.
Reduce the heat to a very low simmer, cover and
cook for 2 hours. Alternatively, pop into an oven
preheated to 150°C/300°F/gas mark 2 for 2 hours.

season

Taste and season with more salt as needed.
Serve with rice or parathas (see page 122).

black
pork
curry

serves ● ● ● ●

prep ◕

cook ○ ◔

ingredients

600g (1lb 5oz) pork, cut
into 2.5-cm (1-in) chunks
2½ Tbsp Sri Lankan curry
powder (see page 35)
3 Tbsp tamarind paste
1 Tbsp freshly ground
black pepper
1 tsp salt
2 Tbsp vegetable oil
2 onions, finely chopped
5cm (2in) ginger, peeled
and minced
4 cloves garlic, minced
1 cinnamon stick
5 cardamom pods

mix

Mix the pork with 2 tablespoons of the curry powder, tamarind paste and freshly ground black pepper, and salt. Set aside.

stir-fry

Heat the oil in a large saucepan, then add the onions, ginger, garlic, cinnamon and cardamom pods and stir-fry on a medium heat for 10 minutes until golden brown and softened.

cook

Add the pork and stir-fry for a further 2–3 minutes, then add 100ml (3½fl oz/7 tablespoons) water. Bring to the boil, then reduce the heat, cover and simmer for 45 minutes.

simmer

Remove the lid and simmer for a further 10 minutes to reduce the sauce, stirring frequently.

season

Taste and season with salt as needed. Sprinkle with the remaining curry powder just before serving.

(vegetable curry)

jackfruit curry

(polos curry)

serves

prep

cook **x2**

ingredients

2 Tbsp vegetable oil
1 onion, finely chopped
2 cloves garlic, finely minced
5cm (2in) ginger, peeled
   and finely minced
10 curry leaves
1 green chilli, deseeded
   and finely chopped
1 Tbsp Sri Lankan curry
   powder (see page 35)
½ tsp ground turmeric
1 tsp salt
2 Tbsp tamarind paste
2 x 230-g (8-oz) cans jackfruit
   (drained weight 600g/1lb 5oz)
400ml (13½fl oz/1⅔ cups)
   coconut milk

stir-fry

Heat the oil in a large saucepan on a medium heat, then add the onion, garlic, ginger, curry leaves and chilli and stir-fry for 10 minutes until golden brown.

boil

Add the curry powder, turmeric and salt and stir-fry for a further minute before adding the tamarind paste. Mix well, then add the jackfruit and coconut milk and bring to the boil.

simmer

Reduce the heat to a low simmer and cover and cook for 2 hours, or until the jackfruit is completely soft and the sauce is rich and dark. Season to taste with salt, then serve with coconut rice (see page 117) or chapattis (see page 123).

31

beetroot curry

ingredients

2 Tbsp vegetable oil
1 Tbsp mustard seeds
1 Tbsp fenugreek seeds
10 curry leaves
1 green chilli, deseeded
   and finely sliced
1 onion, finely chopped
1–2 tsp chilli powder,
   or to taste
500g (1lb 2oz) beetroot (beet),
   peeled and thinly sliced
1 tsp salt
75ml (2½fl oz/5 Tbsp)
   coconut milk

stir-fry

Heat the oil in a large saucepan on a medium heat until very hot. Add the mustard seeds and fenugreek seeds, and as soon as they begin to pop and splutter, add the curry leaves, chilli and onion and stir-fry for 10 minutes until golden brown.

simmer

Add the chilli powder and stir-fry for 1 minute, then add the beetroot. Stir, pour in 400ml (13½fl oz/1⅔ cups) boiling water, add the salt, then cover and simmer for 30 minutes, or until the beetroot is completely soft.

stir

Stir through the coconut milk and simmer, uncovered, for a further 5 minutes. Taste and season with more salt as needed, then serve.

beetroot curry

okra curry

(bandakka curry)

serves

prep

cook

ingredients

4 Tbsp vegetable oil

350g (12¼oz) okra, cut into
    1-cm (½-in) slices

1 tsp mustard seeds

1 small onion, finely sliced

1 tsp ground turmeric

1 Tbsp Sri Lankan curry
    powder (see page 35)

1 red chilli, deseeded
    and finely sliced

100ml (3½fl oz/7 Tbsp)
    coconut milk

juice of ½ lime

1 tsp salt

heat

Heat the oil in a large wok, then add the okra
and stir-fry on a high heat for 5 minutes, or until
lightly golden brown and crisp. Remove with
a slotted spoon and drain on a plate lined with
kitchen paper (paper towel).

stir-fry

Add the mustard seeds, and as soon as they start
to pop, add the onion and stir-fry on a high heat
for 5 minutes until browned. Reduce the heat,
add the turmeric, curry powder and chilli and stir-fry
on a medium heat for a further minute.

season

Return the crisp okra to the pan along with the
coconut milk. Stir well for a further minute, then
season to taste with the lime juice and salt before
serving immediately.

sri lankan pumpkin curry

(wattaka curry)

serves

prep

cook

ingredients

2 Tbsp vegetable oil
1 onion, finely chopped
10 curry leaves
1 green chilli, deseeded
   and finely chopped
2 cloves garlic, finely chopped
1 Tbsp Sri Lankan curry
   powder (see page 35)
1 tsp fenugreek seeds
½ tsp ground turmeric
500g (1lb 2oz) pumpkin or
   butternut squash, cut into
   1.5-cm (½-in) cubes
400ml (13½fl oz/1⅔ cups)
   coconut milk
1 tsp salt
3 Tbsp grated fresh coconut

stir-fry

Heat the oil in a saucepan on a medium heat, then add the onion, curry leaves, chilli and garlic and stir-fry for 10 minutes until golden brown. Add the curry powder, fenugreek seeds and turmeric and stir-fry for a further minute on a low heat.

simmer

Add the pumpkin, coconut milk and salt, stir, then bring to the boil. Cover and simmer for 25–30 minutes until the pumpkin is soft and cooked through.

stir

Stir in the grated coconut and simmer for a further 2–3 minutes. Taste and season with more salt as needed, then serve with rice.

95

sri lankan
pumpkin curry

coconut broth

(kiri hodi)

serves ●●●●

prep

cook

ingredients
1 onion, finely sliced
2 green chillies, deseeded
   and finely sliced
2 cloves garlic, finely sliced
10 curry leaves
½ tsp ground turmeric
½ tsp fenugreek seeds
1 cinnamon stick
400ml (13½fl oz/1⅔ cups)
   coconut milk
juice of 1 lime
1 tsp salt

simmer
Pop the onion, chillies, garlic, curry leaves, turmeric, fenugreek seeds and cinnamon in a saucepan along with 150ml (5fl oz/⅔ cup) water. Bring to the boil, then cover and simmer for 5 minutes.

stir
Add the coconut milk and stir on a medium heat for 2–3 minutes, making sure that it heats through but does not boil.

season
Add the lime juice and salt to taste and serve with string hoppers (see page 33).

potato and coconut curry

(ala kiri hodi)

serves

prep

cook

ingredients

500g (1lb 2oz) potatoes,
  peeled and cut into
  2.5-cm (1-in) chunks
2 Tbsp vegetable oil
1 Tbsp mustard seeds
10 curry leaves
½ tsp ground turmeric
2 green chillies, deseeded
  and finely sliced
1 onion, finely sliced
300ml (10fl oz/1¼ cups)
  coconut milk
1–2 tsp salt

boil

Boil the potatoes in a saucepan of salted water
for 10 minutes until just parboiled, then drain.

stir-fry

Meanwhile, heat the oil in a large saucepan,
then add the mustard seeds, curry leaves,
turmeric and chillies and stir-fry on a medium
heat for a few seconds until the mustard seeds
pop. Add the onion and stir-fry for 5 minutes on
a very low heat until slightly softened.

cook

Add the coconut milk and salt, then bring to the boil.
Add the potatoes and cook for a further 10 minutes
until they are tender. Taste and season with more
salt as needed. Serve with string hoppers (see page
33), steamed white rice (see page 110) or chapattis
(see page 123).

leeks mirisata

serves

prep

cook

ingredients

1 Tbsp Maldive fish
  or fish sauce
2 Tbsp vegetable oil
2 leeks, thinly sliced
1 tsp chilli flakes
½ tsp ground turmeric
1 tsp salt

crush

Crush the Maldive fish in a pestle (if using) and mortar.

stir-fry

Heat the oil in a large wok on a medium heat, then add the leeks and stir-fry for 5 minutes until wilted. Add the chilli flakes, turmeric, salt and Maldive fish or fish sauce. Stir, then cover and cook for 15 minutes on a very low heat.

cook

Remove the lid, stir, then cook, uncovered, for a further 10 minutes until sticky, stirring occasionally. Taste and add salt as needed. Serve hot with rice.

37

thai aubergine curry

(ela batu)

serves ●●●●○
prep ◕
cook ◑

ingredients

2 Tbsp vegetable oil
1 tsp mustard seeds
1 onion, finely sliced
3 cloves garlic, finely chopped
2 green chillies, deseeded
  and finely chopped
5 curry leaves
1 Tbsp Sri Lankan curry
  powder (see page 35)
1 tsp ground turmeric
1 tsp salt
300g (10½oz) Thai or small
  aubergines (eggplants),
  halved
400ml (13½fl oz/1 cup)
  coconut milk
juice of 1 lime

cook

Heat the oil in a large frying pan or wok, then add the mustard seeds and cook on a low heat for 30–40 seconds until they pop.

stir-fry

Add the onion, garlic, chillies and curry leaves and stir-fry for 10 minutes on a medium heat until evenly golden brown. Add the curry powder, turmeric and salt and stir-fry for 1 minute. Add the aubergines and stir-fry for a further 5–6 minutes until softened.

simmer

Add the coconut milk, bring to the boil, then simmer for a further 10 minutes until the aubergines are completely cooked through.

season

Season with the lime juice, then taste and add more salt as needed. Serve hot.

thai aubergine curry

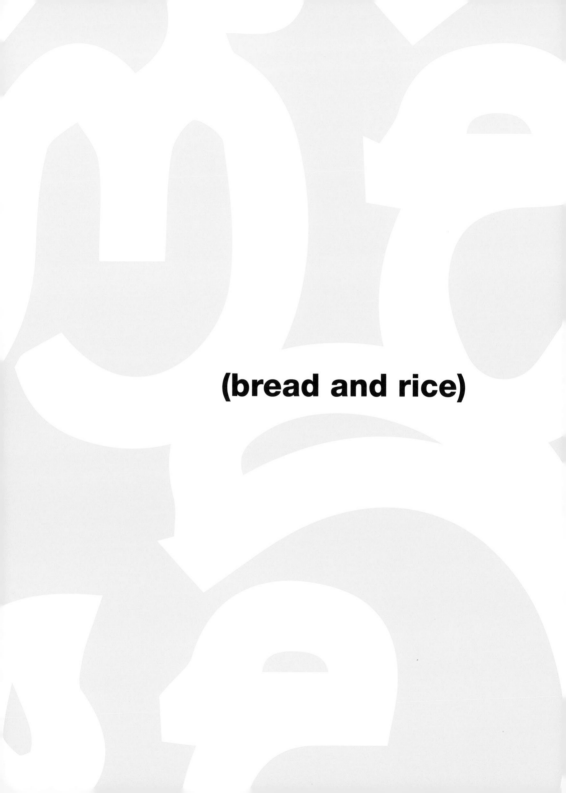

(bread and rice)

steamed white rice

serves

prep

cook

ingredients
200g (7oz/generous 1 cup)
basmati rice, well rinsed

boil
Place the rice and 360ml (12fl oz/1½ cups) water
in a saucepan with a tight-fitting lid and bring
the water to the boil. Stir, then cover immediately
and reduce the heat to its lowest setting.

cook
Cook without removing the lid for 15 minutes.
The rice should have absorbed all the water.

steam
Fluff it through with a fork and leave to steam,
uncovered, for 5 minutes before serving.

sri lankan egg fried rice

serves

prep

cook

ingredients

50g (1¾oz/3½ Tbsp) butter
  or ghee
2 leeks, finely sliced
1 red onion, finely sliced
2 cloves garlic, minced
5cm (2in) ginger, peeled
  and minced
2 eggs, beaten
240g (8½oz/2 cups) cooked
  basmati rice
2–3 Tbsp soy sauce
pinch salt, or to taste

stir-fry

Heat the butter in a wok on a medium heat,
then add the leeks and onion and stir-fry on
a high heat for 5 minutes. Add the garlic and
ginger and stir-fry for a further 2–3 minutes until
the vegetables are softened.

scramble

Add the eggs and stir-fry for 30 seconds until
just scrambled, then add the rice. Stir-fry for 3–4
minutes until the rice is hot all the way through.

season

Season with the soy sauce and salt to taste
and serve hot.

chicken biryani

chicken biryani

ingredients

500g (1lb 2oz) boneless
  chicken thighs, quartered
3 cloves garlic, finely minced
5cm (2in) ginger, peeled
  and finely minced
1 green chilli, deseeded
  and finely chopped
2 tomatoes, finely chopped
1 tsp ground turmeric
1 tsp chilli powder
1 tsp ground cumin
1 tsp ground coriander
3 Tbsp natural yogurt
1 tsp salt

marinate

Mix the chicken thighs with the garlic, ginger, chilli, tomatoes, turmeric, chilli powder, cumin, ground coriander, yogurt and salt. Leave to marinate for 1 hour, or overnight.

stir-fry

Heat the oil in a large frying pan, then add the onions and stir-fry for 10 minutes on a medium heat until golden brown and crisp, then remove half and set aside for later.

simmer

Add the marinated chicken and stir-fry for a further 2–3 minutes. Add 250ml (8½fl oz/1 cup) water, cover, then simmer on a very low heat for 20 minutes until cooked. Season to taste with salt.

par-boil

Five minutes before the chicken is cooked, par-boil the rice in a large saucepan of boiling salted water for 5 minutes.

serves

prep

marinate

cook

2 Tbsp vegetable oil
2 onions, finely sliced
300g (10½oz/1¾ cups)
  basmati rice
40g (1½oz/3 Tbsp) butter,
  melted
2 Tbsp Greek yogurt

layer

Drain the rice well. Pour a quarter of the butter into a fresh saucepan, then add one-third of the rice. Use a slotted spoon to remove half of the cooked chicken and onions from the sauce and flatten over the rice.

cook

Repeat with the rice, butter, chicken and reserved onions and finish with a layer of rice. Pour over the remaining butter, cover tightly in foil, then a lid, then place on a low heat to cook for 30 minutes.

reduce

Meanwhile, reduce the sauce that you cooked the chicken in by half. This should take about 10 minutes on a slow boil. Stir in the Greek yogurt and season to taste. Serve the biryani with the sauce on the side.

coconut rice

(kiribath)

serves

prep

cook

ingredients

200g (7oz/generous 1 cup)
   white short-grain rice,
   well rinsed
400ml (13½fl oz/1⅔ cups)
   coconut milk
1 tsp salt

simmer

Place the rice in a saucepan with 360ml (12fl oz/
1½ cups) water and bring to the boil. Stir, then
cover and simmer on a low heat for 15 minutes
without removing the lid.

cook

Add the coconut milk and salt, stir well, then
cook for a further 15–20 minutes, covered, on a
very low heat until the coconut milk is absorbed.

flatten

Turn the rice out onto a dinner plate and flatten
into a cake. Leave to cool slightly, then cut into
slices or diamonds to serve.

coconut roti

makes

prep

rest

cook

ingredients

250g (9oz/about 1¾ cups)
   plain (all-purpose) flour
80g (3oz/generous 1 cup)
   grated fresh coconut
½ red onion, finey chopped
1 green chilli, deseeded
   and finely chopped
1 tsp salt
1 Tbsp vegetable oil

mix

Mix the flour, grated coconut, onion, chilli and salt together in a large bowl, then add 100ml (3½fl oz/7 tablespoons) water and the oil and work everything together into a stiff, pliable dough. Cover with clingfilm (plastic wrap) and leave to rest at room temperature for 30 minutes.

roll

Divide the dough into 8 equal pieces, then roll each piece into a ball. Flatten and roll into 15-cm (6-in) discs, using a little more vegetable oil to prevent them sticking.

cook

Heat a large heavy-based frying pan on a medium heat and pop 2–3 rotis in the pan in a single layer at a time. Cook for 2 minutes on each side until cooked through. Serve hot.

parathas

makes

prep

rest

cook

ingredients

300g (10½oz/2¼ cups) plain
(all-purpose) flour
½ tsp salt
5 Tbsp ghee or melted butter

mix

Mix the flour and salt together in a large bowl.
Gradually add 2 tablespoons of the ghee and 120ml
(4fl oz/½ cup) water and bring together into a dough.
Knead for 1 minute until it is soft and pliable, then
return to the bowl. Cover with clingfilm (plastic wrap)
and leave to rest at room temperature for 30 minutes.

roll

Divide the dough into 8 equal pieces. Roll each
into a circle 2mm (¹⁄₁₆in) thick, then brush the top
with ghee. Fold in half, brush the top with more
ghee, then fold in half again to form a triangle.
Roll until it is 1mm (¹⁄₃₂in) thick.

cook

Heat a large frying pan on a medium heat until
very hot. Make one paratha at a time and cook
for 1 minute on each side until golden brown in
patches. Serve hot.

chapattis

makes

prep

rest

cook

ingredients

250g (9oz/1¾ cups) wholemeal
(wholewheat) flour, plus extra
for dusting
1 tsp salt
1 Tbsp vegetable oil or ghee

mix

Mix the flour and salt together in a large bowl.
Gradually add 125ml (4fl oz/½ cup) water and the
oil and bring together into a dough. Knead briefly
for 1 minute until it is soft and pliable, then return
to the bowl. Cover with clingfilm (plastic wrap) and
leave to rest at room temperature for 30 minutes.

roll

Heat a large frying pan on a medium heat and
divide the dough into 8 equal pieces. Roll each
out on a floured surface until no thicker than
1mm (⅟₃₂in).

cook

Cook each chapatti for 1 minute on each side
as you roll out the next one. If you have rolled
them thinly and evenly enough, they should puff
up in the pan (but this will take some practice).
Keep warm while you cook the rest. Serve hot.

fermented pancakes

fermented pancakes

(thosai dosa)

ingredients

400g (14oz/2¼ cups) American
   long-grain rice, rinsed
200g (7oz/1 cup) white urad
   dhal lentils, washed
½ tsp fenugreek seeds
1 Tbsp vegetable oil

soak

Place the rice and lentils in separate bowls,
with a pinch of fenugreek seeds in each.
Cover generously with cold water, then leave
to soak for 8 hours, or overnight.

blitz

Drain the water from the lentils and place in a food
processor or blender along with 250ml (8½fl oz/
1 cup) water. Blitz until completely smooth, then
transfer to a bowl.

blend

Place half the soaked rice in the food processor
or blender along with 50ml (1¾fl oz/3 tablespoons)
water and blend until it is very smooth, then add
to the blitzed dhal. Repeat with the remaining rice
and a further 50ml (1¾fl oz/3 tablespoons) water.
Combine the two mixtures together, along with
a further 150ml (5fl oz/⅔ cup) water until a thick
batter forms.

makes

prep

soak over-
night

cook

ferment

Cover the batter with clingfilm (plastic wrap)
and leave to ferment in a warm place overnight,
or until bubbly on top and doubled in size.

chill

Once the batter has fermented, it's ready to
use. You can keep the batter in the fridge,
covered, until you are ready to cook, and up
to 3 days afterwards.

cook

To cook the thosai, heat 1 teaspoon of the oil in
a heavy-based frying pan on a medium heat, then
pour half a ladleful of batter into the centre. Very
quickly, use the base of the ladle to smooth out
the batter into a large circle using circular motions,
as thinly as you can. Increase the heat and cook
for 1 minute on each side until crispy. Repeat with
the remaining batter until the pancakes are all
cooked. They are best eaten straight out of the
pan. Serve with sambhar (see page 42).

(desserts and drinks)

kiri toffee

serves

prep

cook

ingredients
50g (1¾oz/½ cup) cashew nuts
397-g (14-oz) can condensed
   milk
150g (5½oz/¾ cup) caster
   (superfine) sugar
5 cardamom pods, seeds
   only, crushed
25g (1oz/2 Tbsp) unsalted
   butter, plus extra for greasing

toast
Toast the cashews in a frying pan for 5–6 minutes
until golden brown. Cool, then roughly chop.

boil
Heat the condensed milk and sugar together
in a pan, and bring to the boil, stirring. Add the
cashews and cardamom seeds, and boil, stirring,
for 15 minutes on a medium heat until it becomes
very thick, and turns a deep golden brown.

stir
Add the butter, then stir for 5–6 minutes until
the mixture becomes even thicker. It is ready
when it starts to come together in a ball.

cool
Tip into a buttered 18-cm (7-in) square cake
tin and flatten out, using a buttered spatula.
Leave to cool, then cut into squares.

47

coconut pancakes
(wellawahum/pani pol)

makes

prep

cook

ingredients

200g (7oz/1½ cups) plain
  (all-purpose) flour
¼ tsp ground turmeric
¼ tsp salt
2 eggs
250ml (8½fl oz/1 cup) milk
2 cardamom pods, seeds only
2 cloves
¼ cinnamon stick
120g (4¼oz/scant ⅔ cup)
  palm sugar or jaggery
200g (7oz/scant 3 cups)
  grated fresh coconut
1 Tbsp vegetable oil

whisk

Mix the flour, turmeric and salt in a large bowl.
Whisk the eggs with the milk, then gradually pour
into the flour and whisk to form a smooth batter.
Leave to rest at room temperature for 15 minutes.

grind

Grind the cardamom seeds, cloves and cinnamon
stick in a pestle and mortar.

simmer

Tip into a saucepan along with the sugar and 1
tablespoon water. Stir on a medium heat for 2–3
minutes until the sugar has dissolved, then simmer
for 10 minutes. Add the coconut, stir and cook
on a low heat for 5 minutes until thick and syrupy.

cook

Heat the oil in a large frying pan on a medium heat,
then remove most of it with kitchen paper (paper
towel). Pour in 3–4 tablespoons of batter and swirl
to cover the base of the pan. Cook each pancake
for 1 minute on each side. Remove and keep
warm. Repeat with the remaining batter to make
6 pancakes.

roll

Place 2 tablespoons of the filling in each pancake,
and roll up before serving hot.

watermelon, mint and lime juice

serves

prep

ingredients
1 large chilled watermelon,
   roughly cut into chunks
juice of 1 lime
1 handful mint leaves

blitz
Place all the ingredients in a blender or food
processor and blitz until smooth.

strain
Tip the liquid into a sieve set over a bowl, and
use a spoon to sieve the juice out until you can't
get any more juice from the pulp.

chill
Pour into a jug and chill in the fridge for 30 minutes
before serving.

passion fruit lassi (top)
mango lassi (bottom)

passion fruit lassi

serves

prep

ingredients

8 passion fruit, pulp only
500g (1lb 2oz/2⅓ cups)
  natural yogurt
4–5 Tbsp caster (superfine)
  sugar

blitz

Place all the ingredients into a blender, along with 200ml (7fl oz/scant 1 cup) water and blitz until smooth.

chill

Taste and add more sugar as required. Strain into a jug and refrigerate for 30 minutes before serving.

mango lassi

serves

prep

ingredients
3 ripe mangoes, flesh only
500ml (17fl oz/generous
    2 cups) natural yogurt
2 Tbsp caster (superfine)
    sugar

blitz
Place all the ingredients into a blender, along with 250ml (8½fl oz/1 cup) water and blitz until very smooth. Taste and adjust the level of sugar as required, adding a little more water for a thinner consistency if you wish.

chill
Refrigerate for at least 1 hour before serving.

index

Thank you to all the owners, people and staff who allowed us to shoot photographs in the following locations: Sri Lanka (Colombo, Galle, Kandy, Ella and Sigiriya), Kothu Kothu and South Harrow Food & Wine and Best foods.

Note: follow the standard safety tips for deep frying – fill the pan no more than half full with oil, keep it towards the back of the stove, do not leave it unattended, and do not overcrowd the pan, or it will bubble over. Once you have finished frying, turn off the heat and do not attempt to move the pan of oil until it has completely cooled down.

publishing director: Sarah Lavelle
creative director: Helen Lewis
junior commissioning editor: Romilly Morgan
design and art direction: Claire Rochford
recipe developer and food stylist: Rukmini Iyer
photographer: Kim Lightbody
illustrator: Juriko Kosaka
prop stylist: Alexander Breeze
production: Tom Moore, Vincent Smith

First published in 2017 by
Quadrille Publishing
Pentagon House
52–54 Southwark Street
London SE1 1UN
www.quadrille.co.uk
www.quadrille.com

Quadrille is an imprint of Hardie Grant
www.hardiegrant.com.au

Text © 2017 Quadrille Publishing
Photography © 2017 Kim Lightbody
Photography on pages 1, 3, 12, 82, 93, 120, 125,
140–141 & 144 © Romilly Morgan and Rohan Schneider
Illustration © 2017 Juriko Kosaka
Design and layout © 2017 Quadrille Publishing

Cataloguing in Publication Data: a catalogue record
for this book is available from the British Library.

ISBN: 978 184949 962 0

Printed in China